Your Empowering Life Healing Journey

Dara Rabel is an accredited Reiki Master Healer, certified Feng Shui Practitioner and authority on other Healing modalities. Her principal work is Healing on the emotional, mental, physical and spiritual levels.

This book is the culmination of three years of preparation. Two years were then devoted to the writing and illustration to ensure that the words and images were perfect, to facilitate the optimal experience for the reader. Working with Hania, an incredible graphic designer with thirty years experience, was instrumental in presenting the images as an accurate interpretation within a design.

Dara is currently writing her next book on appreciating and enhancing the energy on the deepest levels within us. She sees clients privately for healing and teaching sessions at the 'Soul Life Healing Therapy' and provides clearing and Feng Shui Healing consultations for both home and business.

She lives in Western Canada with her husband and has three grown up children.

SoulLifeHealings@gmail.com

Your Empowering Life Healing Journey

Live your optimum life

Dara Rabel

Resolute Ventures Inc. (of Alberta, Canada)

Your Empowering Life Healing Journey

Live your optimum life

© 2016 Dara Rabel

All rights reserved. This book or any portion thereof may not be reproduced or used in any manner whatsoever without the express written permission of the author or publisher except for the use of brief quotations in a book review. Any unauthorized use of its contents is strictly prohibited.

Limit of liability/disclaimer of warranty. With respect to all information provided in this book, the author and publisher make no warranties of any kind, express or implied (including warranties of suitability for a particular purpose) and shall not be liable for any loss arising out of use of this information, including without limitation any indirect or consequential damages. The information presented in this book is as a service to our readers of the best intention for improvement.

ISBN-13: 978-0995268401

ISBN-10: 0995268401

Printed in the United States of America

First Edition, Paperback, 2016

Design and illustrations © 2016 Hania Oleksiuk

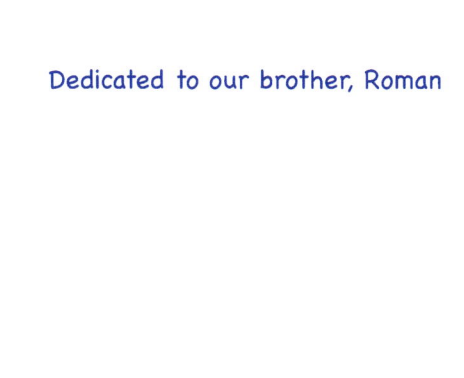

This book prompted me numerous times to be written. The images would insistently reveal themselves to me in a dream or during a meditation, but I did not know the best way for it to be written. This was then also revealed, when I read an article about the increasing number of incidents of cancer, especially in children. I then knew exactly how it should be written and began to write it.

I encourage the reader to follow the journey in this book perceptively and diligently. Results will not happen overnight. It takes dedication to advance. Believe that good results can happen for you; truly believe that this is what you want in your life and the results are limited only by the limits of your belief.

If you are presently under the care of a physician, continue to attend your medical appointments. I have great respect for the medical profession and began my own training in the medical field before discovering and following the path of energy healing.

Allow the pure energy you will receive to create your view of the world around you with different eyes, with a different heart. Enjoy all the moments of your life. Treasure the people around you. This does not mean that you will not encounter challenges in your life; it does mean that you will be better equipped with superior tools to handle them on the mental, emotional, physical and spiritual levels.

Thank you to my sister, Hania, for her untiring patience in listening to precisely how the images should appear; to design the pages to present the images and colors at their purest, as only her meticulous work and understanding of me could accomplish. This book would not be the beautiful work without her efforts. It was also wonderful to have worked on this project together.

Thank you to the encouragement of my family, especially my amazing husband. All of you always believed in me, so how could I not believe in myself!

Dara Rabel
September 2016

'Your Empowering Life Healing Journey' presents the prospect of healing. It is the reader who determines the infinite value to be received from each page. This is the journey to reclaim the appreciation of the essence of our life, in its most pure, original form. This book is a flowing series of images and colors, connected together by a remarkably unique technique, embodying the power of life healing, which is instilled into each page of this book. This process is so unique, that the author has needed to give it a name, 'Soul Oneness Power'.

These images will enable this remarkable purity to be tapped and revitalized, to deliver to us the benefits on an emotional, physical, mental or spiritual level, significantly improving our life. Once attained, at any stage in our life, we can continue to reach this empowering energy by viewing the images and colors and to draw upon this energy, so it will be continually present for us. This is a journey presenting only the very pure and positive and there are no concerns to resist it.

The pure images and dynamic colors in this book create the ability to connect the uncomplicated level of a mind to a new, higher level of vibrational energy, never accessed on the conscious level. These images are visually simple, but establish this intricate link very powerfully. The presented images were received during several deep meditations and journeys. Subsequent meditations brought deeper revelations of the images.

As children, we view an object intuitively, with an accepting mind. As adults, we have grown up into the flurry of daily life and distanced ourselves from this ability, embedding it deep within ourselves, where it can no longer be retrieved. Our questioning minds have probably become encumbered with everyday routines, very constricted and incompatible with the limitless freedom of our mind, enhanced at a higher, spiritual level. We all have the intuition, the power to heal ourselves. We need to regain this capability, nurturing it to serve our life on a profound level to bring us this magnificent and restorative effect on all aspects of our life.

The images and colors are energy. Everything is energy. We are energy. The energy of the images, the colors and the energy of our body can thus come together, creating a oneness. These images and colors inspire that ability. The first sequence of eight colors, based on vibrations, is at a superior intensity. The second sequence of seven colors is at a greatly elevated vibrational plane from the first sequence, being infused with a light we have never before known, a light of the supreme level. This vibrational nature created by the combination of the images and colors enables them to be transmitted to our spiritual level.

When colors are dynamic, they are awe-inspiring, making everything around become more magnificent, filling us with immensely positive emotions and well-being. This is also true of the energy within us. We need to bring these highly vibrant colors through the images to the inside of us, keeping them as brilliant as possible, so that everything within us and in our space will be encompassed in this radiance and enable us to reach our optimum in life.

These images carry specific colors, which express serenity, clearing and healing, interconnected to guide you through your journey. People are intuitively attuned to this level of imagery. As you read the elements of this journey, take the time to see and accept each image. Clear the mind, so that the essence can be deeply appreciated. Stay with the image for a while. With focus, it is easily possible to attain this empowering level, united with the images represented in this book, and to enjoy the powerful offering it brings into your life.

'Your Empowering Life Healing Journey' is intended for people who require healing, whether it be on an emotional, physical, mental or spiritual level. It is respectfully offered to those people experiencing cancer. The final pages of this book complete the imagery and offer your unique healing. It simply needs to be welcomed, received and accepted.

This is your journey of empowering healing.

A stone bridge spans a narrow stream. The stream flows along, lapping around small rocks. The water is clear and reflects the sunlight in bursts of sparkles here and there. Made of uneven stones, the bridge mirrors the sun in a range of reds, with no two tones being the same. The colors twinkle in the sunshine, changing progressively from a light pink, to crimson, then to a pure red. Gradually, the bridge becomes bathed in an intensity of luminous red, radiating out onto the dancing water. The bridge looks like it is made of translucent red glass. The stream,

Sense the pure air, gently moving around you

flowing beneath it, reflects the bursts of crimsons and reds. The water holds and then releases into the air each spurt of color. As the streaming water passes underneath the bridge, the burbling sound of the water echoes against the stones, creating a deep, full resonance of a breadth of tones. The sound of the flowing water is mesmerizing. Its perpetual gurgling and rippling is the only sound heard, creating a serenity. This color and sound are entrancing, calming. The scene appears as if it is in a painting, never before seen in the real world.

Dara Rabel

Walking along the grassy bank of the stream to the bridge, you hear the gurgling water. Kneeling down, you reach down and put your hands into the water. The water is cool and fresh. You make a scoop with your hands, hold the water, and then splash it onto your face, sending droplets sprinkling in all directions. Feeling the effect of the fresh water almost taking away your breath, you laugh. You scoop more water from the stream to trickle onto your face. You savor the refreshing effect. You see a donkey approaching and stand up. His coat appears almost orange in the

Inhale the purity, yours to have

gleaming sunshine. He stops close by, nodding his head higher several times. Interpreting this as a "hello", you say "Hello" to him. He bows his head to begin to graze the grass, where there are droplets of the fresh water. You stand at the bank, watching him. The donkey raises his head, then slowly plods closer, stopping near you. You reach out to stroke his back. His hair coat is so velvety, that it is hard to stop patting him. Nodding his head, the donkey continues to amble along the bank of the stream, his coat seeming more orange against the red bridge.

Dara Rabel

There is a peace. There is no sound from the flowing water of the stream. You sense this tranquility. Past the bridge, a baby elephant lifts his trunk in greeting, but makes no sound. You marvel at the elephant with delight, as he is very small, a baby, very different from the gigantic creature of his mother, who stands patiently beside him. The mother elephant moves her trunk to the stream, drawing in some pure, clear water. She lifts up her trunk and sprays out the water in a fine drizzle of yellow droplets over the baby elephant. The baby elephant also lifts

Release all which does not serve you, exhale

his trunk in a comical attempt to imitate his mother. This gentle scene is very touching. A yellow haze of droplets lands on the grass, transforming those lush green grass blades into sparkling yellow. You want to pat the baby elephant's back, but are hesitant because he is standing so close to his protective mother. The mother elephant, appreciating this, lifts her trunk and moves it towards you, gently blowing air over your hair. Laughing, you pat the trunk and stroke the baby elephant's smooth back.

A jester, his clothing of vibrant green and turquoise, approaches the mother elephant and touches her trunk. In response, the mother elephant lightly encircles the jester's waist with her trunk. He steps towards the baby elephant and strokes his head. Noticing you, the jester moves gently away from the elephant, removes his top hat and bows down low in a greeting. You respond by inclining your head politely. The jester nods in acknowledgement. He places his hat on the ground and removes a globe from it. The color of this globe is as vivid

Walk forward, gradually, lightly through the grass

a green as the jester's clothing. He sets the globe on the grass. Green light begins to lift from the globe, swirling in increasing circles and rising upwards. The higher they ascend, the greater the intensity of green light is produced. Enthralled, you watch the swirls, lifting and twirling, higher and higher into the air. Whirls of green light intertwine with each other, forming curls and shapes, each one very unique in design. You recognize familiar shapes. Several patterns merge to form a tapestry of hues of green that is very magnificent to observe.

Dara Rabel

You begin to feel yourself rising from the ground, hovering above the globe on the circles of light, which transform from green to a pure blue. Watching this in awe, you drift effortlessly upwards, encircled by the pure blue light. You welcome this new feeling of floating as quite exhilarating. Peace. You enjoy your weightlessness, breathing in the very pure air. The spans of pure blue sky, the green land and the blue water lie before you. This tranquility is a new sentiment for you, but you welcome and savor its soothing effect.

On the ground, the jester places his

Enjoy the warmth of the sun bathing your face

hands over the globe and the swirls begin to whirl, changing his costume from green to blue. You are brought gently back to the ground. Sensing a strong, new energy within you, you feel elated. The jester picks up the globe and extends it towards you. Understanding that you may touch the globe, you place both hands on its shiny surface. A small swirl of deep royal blue is released and drifts to the top of your head, empowering you with the now familiar feeling of serenity. Holding the globe, the jester nods a farewell and skips happily away.

Dara Rabel

Your attention is diverted from your wonderful journey with the jester to the image of a frog, hopping towards you. He is a large frog, not green, as you would expect, but a deep royal blue, an indigo color. He wears a crown of the same indigo color. He stops beside you and you notice that he is as big as you. He inclines his head. As he does so, his crown emits a burst of indigo light, which lingers around you. He points to his back, where he has a small carpet. Understanding that the frog is inviting you to take a ride, you climb up onto the frog's back. As you do so, you

Hear the sounds of nature, gently lulling you into relaxation

feel yourself engulfed in the warm indigo light. The frog hops effortlessly along a small, grassy hill for a short distance. You are not holding onto the frog, but are quite safe, with each gentle hop of the frog. The frog springs back to the bank and waits patiently. Alighting from the frog's back, you see a small trail of indigo light follow and softly envelope you. You are overwhelmed with enthusiasm and find yourself hugging the frog's neck. He stands good-naturedly. An indigo light bathes the hug.

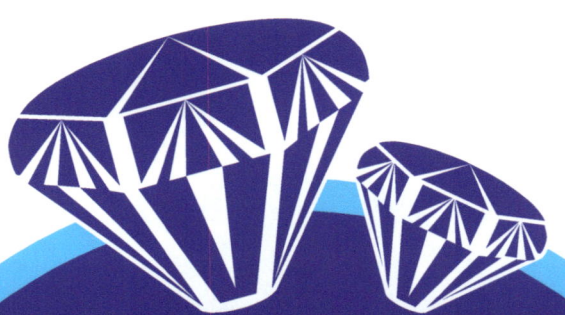

The frog removes his crown and places it on the ground. A beam of white light shines from it into the sky, then returns as a beam of brilliant violet light. This violet light spans out and spreads over the ground, turning into sparkling crystals of deep violet. You feel an eagerness to approach the crystals and examine them, but are respectful and wait patiently. Understanding your intention, the frog nods to you. You hurry excitedly to the crystals and pick one up cautiously. The violet color is so beautiful, so pure, unlike any color you have ever

Hear the water lapping, flowing, ebbing, bringing purity

seen. Holding the crystal lightly in cupped hands, you gaze intently at it. You sense the same feeling of serenity you had felt when you were floating. You place your face closer to the crystal, which emits a wisp of violet light, bathing your face in tenderness. The frog motions from the crystals to your pocket. You place the crystal into your pocket. Placing your hand over your pocket, you pat it gently and see a swirl of violet light rise from underneath your hand. You feel so proud to own this precious source of violet light.

The frog hops towards a huge, ancient chair under a tree. You follow him there. The great chair throws a shading of pink over the grass. Walking in this lush grass, you are surprised at the sight of a chair under a tree, since you perceive it to be a throne. The chair has violet upholstery embroidered with magenta threads and is decorated with pink brocade. The frog stretches his front leg in the direction of the throne, while looking at you. Accepting his invitation, you move towards the throne. The frog stoops down at the foot of the throne and you step

You are safe, you are strong, you are resilient

lightly onto his back and seat yourself into the huge throne. A delight overcomes you as you place your hands on the arms of the throne, feeling the plush fabric against your skin. Running your hand over the pink brocade, you feel special. You feel distinguished. It is as though you are empowered by all the ancient wisdom and vision of the ancient throne. You straighten your back, holding your head up high. You smile. How honored you feel to be sitting in this magnificent throne. Dignity. The frog stands up and bows to you. Respect.

From the ornate throne, you see a huge elephant carrying a passenger, a young boy, in the howdah on his back. The howdah is barely visible, since it is made of a clear material, so translucent that it is practically invisible. It almost seems to you that the little boy is floating in mid-air. The massive, gentle creature places his huge feet silently on the ground, as he makes his way towards the throne. At the throne, he stoops down, enabling his rider to jump off. You alight from the throne seat to welcome the boy. He beams a huge, friendly smile and

See the sun, the grass, the water, inhale, exhale

waves. You return the wave. He feels to you like someone you already know and like. Since the elephant is still kneeling, you take the opportunity to stroke his head. The elephant lifts his trunk in acknowledgement and places it gently on your shoulder. Leaning your head against the elephant's head, you absorb the tenderness and the compassion. The boy bows his head to show his appreciation to the elephant for bringing him to this place. The huge elephant gets up from the ground and waits, standing nobly.

Dara Rabel

You notice that the young boy is wearing a wide belt. Observing this, he proudly removes his belt. It is a wide strap, embedded with many jewels of orange and white, which twinkle, capturing deeper hues of orange. It takes your breath away to see the splendid light dance from jewel to jewel. He rocks it gently, so that the sunlight reflects from the many jewels, cascading in a symphony of light. One jewel emits a ray of orange light onto your cheek. It leaves a warm sensation and you smile as you touch your cheek. The boy holds the belt aloft,

Accept your rejuvenated energy, the exhilaration

causing the jewels to sparkle and radiate rays of dazzling orange light. You are immersed in looking at the varied orange hues of the jewels. It makes the boy feel unique and very exceptional. He laughs. You laugh too, sharing this wonderful spectacle. He extends his arms, offering you the belt. You accept it with an inclination of your head. He smiles and approaches the elephant, who kneels down to allow him to climb into the howdah. The elephant stands up. You watch the boy riding the giant, gentle creature, as it ambles towards the bridge.

While gazing at the bejeweled belt, you realize you have just been given a remarkable gift. You see the top hat on the ground and taking the belt, you roll it up and place it inside. A haze of pale gold drifts up and surrounds the hat, flowing gently around it. As you observe it, you sense the scenery around you changing. A small stream appears, flowing towards the main stream. Trees emerge, some adorned with pale gold blossom and some bearing brightly colored fruit. The leaves on the trees are round and golden, reflecting sparkles of brilliance. Some

Purifying your breathing, purifying your body

fruit falls from the branches onto the ground, opening up in a haze of pale gold light. Your eyes grow wide, as you witness this miracle of nature, happening around you. When the landscape has become filled with trees, blossom and fruit, you detect the sweet fragrance of the blossom, which fills your senses gradually. Picking up a piece of fruit, you taste it. Its sweet juice quenches your thirst. Reaching up to the tree branches, you pick a golden leaf. Its texture is velvety, yet it reflects a pale golden light from its surface. You place it in your pocket.

Dara Rabel

You hear the sound of the bubbling water of the stream, as it flows around rocks. Approaching the stream, you take out a rock close to the bank. You turn it and see that it has the colors of lilac and pink. As you turn it more, the lilac and pink colors become more vibrant. You lay this rock on the bank and reach into the stream to retrieve another two rocks. One by one, you turn the two rocks in your hands, creating an intense lilac color on their surface. You gather all three rocks together and as they contact, a tall, lilac flare is released,

The water laps at your feet, breathe deeply

causing you to gasp. The lilac light descends softly over you creating a feeling of peace, engulfing and bathing you. This empowered feeling then transforms, becoming a love for everyone and everything you have ever known. You have never felt such a compelling emotion. One by one, you place the rocks into the flowing stream. All the rocks in the stream are transformed into vibrant lilac hues from the three rocks. This spectacle is very captivating and you find yourself mesmerized by the transformation of the water into these exquisite colors.

As if emerging from a trance, you shake your head. You move towards a tree to sit down in its shade and relax. The shade, cast by the tree, is a blue color, turning progressively into violet blue. You close your eyes and run your hand through the grass, into this violet blueness. Drawn by its coolness, you take a single blade of grass, examine the water droplets on it and taste one. It tastes so sweet, yet a flavor you cannot identify. You laugh at first when you find yourself eating the blade of grass. The flavor is exquisite, so you take more. With each bite, it fills your

The water flows to you, bringing you purification, refinement

body with a contentment, a fulfillment. The water droplets on the grass blades quench your thirst. The skin of your hands, having touched the grass, feels very smooth and flawless. Seeing how soft the grass made your hands feel, you take a blade and brush it lightly against your cheek. Your cheek becomes rosy, glowing and with soft skin. You take another blade of grass and apply it to your other cheek, which also turns rosy and smooth. Your face is glowing with a deep radiance.

Leaning back against the huge tree, you rest and let your hands sink into the cool grass. Your hand touches an unusual texture and you look down to see a daisy nestled in the grass. Bending down, you look closely into the grass to observe the daisy with its pale gold center and clear petals. Your face comes closer towards it, so that your nose can determine if the flower has any fragrance. Before your nose is even close to the daisy, you breathe in the most subtle and refined scent. You continue to inhale this delicate perfume, filling your body with its

Inhale, inhale, welcome, receive, accept

pure, delicate freshness. Plucking this daisy from the grass, you put it into the top of your clothing, so that you can continue to savor the fragrance, which flows gently over your face. Leaning against the tree, you find yourself recalling all the wonderful emotions of your journey: peace, serenity, harmony, love. You ponder a favorite memory of your journey. There are so many, that it is challenging to choose a single one and you simply accept that you have many extraordinary memories. You certainly consider yourself honored to have experienced such a journey.

You feel perfect. You stand up and observe the creatures and elements, which you had met and seen on your journey, approaching you, merging more and more into each other. All the shapes and colors whirl together, blending, iridescent, upwards, lighter, until they form a collection of magnificent colors, in harmony with each other, creating a oneness. This band of merged colors draws closer to you and encircles you. You feel yourself hovering slightly above the ground. The color band gently raises you, as you float towards a hill. You feel the pleasant

You are content, relaxed, whole, pure

caress of the color band, as you are lowered onto the elevated ground. At the crown of your head is a glow of lilac light, gently embracing your face and hair. You are filled with a profound sense of wellbeing. One portion of the pattern of colors continues to swirl around you. The other segment forms a vast, magnificent, lilac blue mountain range at your back. The colors around you blend more, becoming white. It is a pure, white light, encircling you perfectly. How incredible! You are experiencing the most amazing feeling of true harmony.

As the colors recede, the bridge, the trees, the rocks, the daisies and the water are visible again. Their colors are more vibrant than when you first saw them. The sound of a chorus of songbirds fills the air. The landscape becomes bathed in a pale golden light from the sky. You look around you and marvel at this perfect landscape. You have welcomed these extraordinary events, these unique emotions and have received their gifts. Recognizing that you are privileged to have been presented with the features of this journey, you feel honored and greatly inspired.

You are perfect, complete, a oneness

You sense a unique sentiment arising in your being, a unification of serenity, compassion, gratitude and wellbeing. Accepting this empowering emotion, you wish to continuously draw on it. You do not want it to ever end.

It does not end